WHISPERS

"I want to whisper poetically in your ear"

Charlotte Wright

Copyright © 2016 Charlotte Wright

All rights reserved.

No part of this book or cover may be used or reproduced, scanned, or distributed in any printed or electronic form without the written permission of the author except in the case of brief quotations in critical articles and reviews.

Publisher: Charlotte Wright

ISBN: 978-0692661543 (sc)

This book is dedicated to my first love.

Katherine Bluitt Wright.

Mom

You remain the most

influential representation of love.

Contents

"A WHISPER TO HIS EAR" 1

"IT COULD BE THE WAY" 2

"KING" 4

"YEARNING" 5

"PITCHER OF LOVE" 5

"LONGED FOR YOU" 6

"I KNOW YOU LOVE ME" 8

"FOREVER" 9

"GPS" 9

"MAN, I WANT TO" 10

"I FELT YOU" 11

"HOPE" 12

"BEAUTIFUL TIME" 12

"LET MY LOVE TAKE CARE OF YOU" 13

"BECAUSE I LOVE YOU" 14

"DEAREST HEART" 16

"PRETEND" 17

"THIS TONGUE" 18

"UGLY" 19

"YOU" 20

"IF" 21

"COME, SIT DOWN" 22

"WORDS" 23

"PHENOMENAL YOU ARE" 24
"WHEN I SAY" 26
"ONLY ONE I NEED" 26
"RANDOM THOUGHTS" 27
"A CONVERSATION BETWEEN LOVERS" 28
"SCENT OF LOVE" 29
"SAY MY NAME" 30
"BY CANDLELIGHT" 32
"I FIND MYSELF WEAK" 33
"AFTERSHOCKS" 34
"I'LL KEEP IT" 35
"IS IT JUST ME" 36
"A BEAUTIFUL THING" 38
"HOW DID YOU GREET YOUR LOVE?" 39
"I FANTASIZE OF AUTUMN NIGHTS" 40
"BAD BOY" 41
"GROCERY STORE BLISS" 42
"SOMETHING" 43
"I CRAVE" 44
"WITH A KISS" 45
"YOUR LOVE" 46
"I AM" 47
"HOW SWEET WAS THE KISS YOU ASK?" 48
"HIS ROSE" 48
"HOW" 49

"WHEN LOVERS HANDS MEET" 49

"LOVE'S WISH" 50

"PLEASURE" 52

"HAVE YOU EVER?" 53

"WHAT IF WE TOOK THIS CHANCE?" 54

"CHOCOLATE LAND" 55

"I KNEW" 56

"CONFESSIONS FROM THE KITCHEN" 56

"I NEED YOU" 57

"BEAT YOUR CHEST BABY" 58

"THERE ARE TIMES" 60

"TOUCH" 62

"THE RAIN, THAT'S WHEN I WANT YOU THE MOST 63

"THIS MAN, THIS KING" 64

"SNOW GLOBE" 66

"ONE DAY" 67

"NO THANK YOU, I'M FULL" 68

"MY PRECIOUS" 69

"LET'S SLEEP IN SORTA" 70

"LEGS, HIPS AND THIGHS" 71

"JUST AS I AM" 72

"JUST PUT IT IN" 73

"I WANT SOME MORE" 74

"INSIDE OUR LOVE" 75

"I MISS YOU" 76

"EMOTIONALLY SAFE" 78
"HIS HOME" 79
"CONFESSIONS FROM THE COUCH" 79
"HIS CHEST" 80
"SANCTUARY" 80
"ECSTASY" 81
"DEVOUR" 81
"DELICIOUS KISS" 82
"DEPTH" 82
"WE DON'T HAVE TO TAKE OUR CLOTHES OFF" 83
"SAVING HER HERO" 84
"SUCCESSFUL" 84
"HOPE AND FAITH" 85
"MY KING, MY LOVE" 86
"NOBODY" 87

Special

Acknowledgement

My Google Plus folks.

CWright Thoughts followers.

Thank you for being my first audience.

Whispers

"A Whisper To His Ear"

Something lovely happened when
I whispered in his ear
I wrote a novel to his soul
Filling his mind with chapters of us
I could feel him submerge in every word
Between the oohh's and aahh's he drowned in our love
Whispering to his heart
He is my destined King
Freeing the world from his shoulders
Illustrating my desires to look out for him
Bathing his mind in security
As I whisper in his ear
Stroking his ego with, yes baby
He ate up every whispered pledge eagerly

Charlotte Wright

"It Could Be The Way"

You cruise through my soul leaving solid rhythms I dance to
Touching the earth within me as I glide through your universe

It could be the way
You sprinkle my insecurities in courage
Realizing we all have them, it's just the beauty in imperfection

It could be the way
You sing me victorious songs
Designed only for my heart

It could be the way
You speak a language birthed from respect
There's never a moment I don't know
I'm your lady

Whispers

It could be the way
Your lips rendezvous with mine
Leaving no secret of what you feel inside

It could be the way
You take me apart
Leaving every inch of my skin
Begging and hungry for more

It could be the way
You came at me from the start
The intentions you had just pure on your part
Leaving games for boys and big things for grown men

Charlotte Wright

"King"

The defender of my heart

Wearing courage

Around your neck

You roam my jungle

Unwaveringly

Amidst its thickness

Your roar is sweet poetry

Heard throughout my depths

Crowned by faith

Dipped in strength

You are King

The endangered kind

Yet you walk untouched

Thirsty to leave your mark on me

"Yearning"

Yearning to languish

In your arms

To feel you so deep

You impregnate my desires

Breathing you in as

You pull me closer

You slay my mind with every kiss

"Pitcher Of Love"

We pour our all

In this pitcher of us

Steering the depths

Of all our emotions

Months turn to years

As we savor the taste

Put into our pitcher of love

Charlotte Wright

"Longed For You"

I have longed for you

Longed for you

Longed for you

Longed for you

Longed for your

Rugged hands to soften

On my skin

Longed for your scent

Of masculinity

To paralyze the

Delicacy in my mind

Longed for the depth

In your voice to

Command my back

To arch seductively

Whispers

Longed for your thoughts
To mingle with mine
Creatively
I tend to feel you
Graze my insides
With love
With oomph
With the same type of
Longing too

Charlotte Wright

"I Know You Love Me"

The way you massage my mind with confidence and love

You lay hands on me that say you'd never get enough

Holding my heart like a newborn

I know you love me

I know you love me with your everything

Slow dancing with my heart on uneven grounds

The way you reach for me and not just physically

Pulling my mind toward you gently

Kissing my tears just to see me happy again

I know you love me

The way you live in my smile

Amongst the fools, I am sound

I know you love me

It's in the way you summon my lips

Your whole name is tattooed along my hips

You've invested in my everything

I know you love me

"Forever"

I'd love to give

You joy forever

So you could display

Your innocence again

To hear you speak

With words freed from chains

To hug the child deep down inside

Let him know it's safe to love again

"GPS"

When we get lost

Let's enter our hurts

Into GPS and find the love in us

Never giving up like the voice in my GPS

Rerouting and Rerouting

To get us to our destination

Charlotte Wright

"Man, I Want To"

Take you to paradise
Let you simmer in my passion
Wake senses muted by hurt
Wrap you with my intense love

Man, I want to just lap you up
Dress you in my admiration
Lace your mind with loyalty

Man, I want to take you there
Over and over with a loud touch
Make you erupt with emotions
With thoughts of us

Man, I want to
Wake to your warmth on my back
After long nights of bending, kissing and unleashing love
Man, I want to put you on repeat,
Play you all day until you beg for sweet mercy

"I Felt You"

I felt you tip toe across my skin
With the tenderness of love
I felt you waltzing in my dreams
Kissing my happy ever afters
I felt you outline my heart
With your very own super strength
I felt you breathe a promise of forever
On to my lips
I felt you speak softly into my ears
You'd always be mine

He pulled her in, held her tight,
And whispered in her ear
You're the beautiful distraction for my tortured heart

Charlotte Wright

"Hope"

In his arms

He in mine

We share the magnitude of this word

Hope

I hope to show you

Your worth in my heart

I hope the loudness of my heart doesn't render you deaf

To love you is to hope in

All the beauty life brings

"Beautiful Time"

It's as if I hold time in my hands

When you are in my arms

I thank the life

That our past had laid

Smiling so sweetly to the future

That my eyes gently giggle

"Let My Love Take Care Of You"

Let my love walk with you

Taking steps blindfolded by trust

Guiding us through life's unforeseen

Let my love take care of you

Let my love warm you through winters

Shade you through summers

Be your umbrella in spring

Let my love be your smile

Showing up and showing out when you

Need it the most

Feeding your soul everywhere you go

Let my love write romance throughout your skin

My lips and fingernails doodle only with passion

Let my love erase all life's infractions

Let my love comfort you

Holding and hugging your flaws and imperfections

Let my love live in your heart,

Flourish in your mind and take your hand

Charlotte Wright

"Because I Love You"

Because I love you
I kiss the words flowing off my lips
With great intent
To have them ripple through you
Giving your heart a massage and
Your mind emancipation
Because I love you
I feed you a meal full of nutrition
The only sweetness is an overdose of my affection
Because I love you
I sit in your church
Meditating on your sermon
Walking beside you straight to heaven

Whispers

Because I love you
To verbally tell you is just me being lazy
But to show you I'd sweat and never tire
From that exercise
Because I love you
The proof would only show
As we hold each other high for a lifetime

Charlotte Wright

"Dearest Heart"

When you are near, I'm frozen in time
Wishing to repeat our beginning again
Your words I hug tightly as you speak
To love you is a blessing, to keep you near is my one true prayer
Dearest heart
You are loved, by a woman who honors your Ma and Pa
They gifted me with your precious love
Your heart sings to mine giving it a beat
Dearest heart
You've captured me with your simplicity

When my eyes saw flaws
When my insecurities won that day
Through it all
He painted me beautiful

"Pretend"

Close your eyes, free your mind of anything blue
Pretend I'm there
You've pulled me in just a bit closer
Can you feel my heart racing, then slowing down
Because it's in familiar territory
Just hold me tight with those big safe arms
Pretend there's nowhere else to be, just here in your atmosphere
Kissing me right above my eyes,
My forehead then consuming my lips
Just simple yet dramatic kisses and touches
Nothing else could compare to the language of our lips
The loudness in our touches with every embrace
Pretend I'm there in your space
Entangled in the most passionate way,
Clothed but naked, drenched in desire
The absolute best feeling in the world
Is shared between you and me
Just two hearts whispering with no fear

Charlotte Wright

"This Tongue"

This tongue desires to speak of love
To say such things as, you remind me
Of, sipping lemonade on grandma's porch
Atop the hills and prairie lands of a shaded Texas field

This tongue desires to say you are my everything
The water to my skin, the vitamins to my heart,
The circulation of my soul
Like Katt William's says Everything!!

This tongue longs to build you up
Tell you, your pride stimulates my mind
To tell you I adore the man you are

This tongue longs to whisper such sweetness in your ear
To lick your mind with passion and devotion
To tell every vein and nerve you have my attention
This tongue can do so much
What it will never do is break you down

Whispers

"Ugly"

You make me feel ugly
You just put me on a shelf
No polishing or waxing just
Collecting dust from the silent stares
Once I was your trophy
Oh how much love you showed for me
Now I feel much like your history
You make me feel ugly
I have vivid memories of
The things you use to do
The verbal language you once shared
Dressing my mind with flirtatious care
Now I'm starving for a sign
That you still love me

Charlotte Wright

"You"

You are the dream so sweet
I gain mental weight every time I drift
Your security soars me above the clouds
You drench me in pleasure
Even with brick walls and pavement between us
You are the definition
Of how love can bloom in every type of weather
A King unknown but reign supreme in my presence
You, you and you rotate inside the soul
That houses the flesh and skeletal
You are the truce between my heart and mind
The peace that sits just beneath my skin

"The most beautiful words he told me were
Goodnight and good morning"

Whispers

"If"

If I allowed you to mingle with my lips
Could you interpret the language they hiss?
Could you converse a dialect of your own?

If I allowed you to polish my skin, would you,
Could you lather it in passion?

If I allowed you to gaze into my eyes
Could your true intentions hypnotize mine?

Could you build a village of love, a valley of trust?
If I gave over my heart

"Joy is fire in your soul
Feel it and let the flames engulf you"

Charlotte Wright

"Come, Sit Down"

Come

Sit down

I promise you

A divine adventure on love's cloud

Bring me your hurts

And I shall caress them

Sing to me your dreams

And I'll kiss them with my faith

Empty your tears in my bucket of hope

I promise you

I'll catch them every time

I'll whisper to your heart, "this is where you'll always find me"

Come, sit down

I know it's been quite the journey

Love is not lost

In this union it shall always rise

Whispers

"Words"

See there is no words in existence that could explain
How much I need you
If I stopped and paused for a moment
I can hear you beat
See there's no way to definitively show
How much I support thee
However if I caught you
When you fell and said things like I got you,
Well that's just a mere pattern of our destiny
See there is possibly no way to prove my devotion to you
Time could tell so much if we jump in and submerge
See what I'm trying to say is I love thee
I rather show you for words yes
Even words from a poet are only simple letters
That need action and desire to breathe

Charlotte Wright

"Phenomenal You Are"

Like sun rays breaking through clouds
The hint of rain above Texas skies
The sun hiding behind Chinaberry trees
You are phenomenal
Like the fascination of rainbows
The beauty of butterflies kissing lilies
The joy a child feels amongst a merry go round
The wisdom found in an elderly male
You baby, yes you are phenomenal
To be loved by you is the opportunity to breathe
To smile the second I awake
You are the peace found in a prayer
The mind blowing sentence to a lyricist

Whispers

The beat to a double platinum hit
You are a phenomenal man
Dipped in strength and bronzed in courage
Mmm you baby you are phenomenal
To be in your presence is to know I am loved
To be by your side is to know I am Queen
You are purpose, You are phenomenal

Charlotte Wright

"When I Say"

I love you

I have placed you

Inside my soul

Inside where pure emotions roam

When I say

I love you

I have placed you amongst my

Beautiful throne

To love, support and watch our kingdom grow

"Only One I Need"

In the silence of my mind

When words mute from my tongue

As love fills up my lungs

You are all I breathe

The only one I need

Whispers

"Random Thoughts"

Urges to be

Engulfed by you

Wrapped in

Your thoughts

Covered by

Your desires

I have random thoughts of you

Leg entwined

With yours

Nibbling all across

Your chest

You gazing

As I undress

Mumbling I love you as we caress

Mmm, I have random thoughts of you

Charlotte Wright

"A Conversation Between Lovers"

Hello my dear

How's your heart today?

Did you think of me as I did you?

I have food cause I feel your hunger

Allow me to replenish you with a simple kiss

Dearest love

How are you?

My heart is joyous

Beating to your touch, your terminology,

Your acts of gentle love

Reflections of you come silently, quietly beside me

As I dance throughout my day

I always know you're there because the ease in my breathes

Can you feel my hunger?

I'm full just knowing you feel it too

Therefore I shall not starve

A kiss from you my love is like a double edged sword

It thrills me fully mentally but slows me to a crawl

"Scent of Love"

I want to absorb the scent of his mind
To exhale slowly the desires he has for us
I want to be diluted by his passion
To taste his soul upon my lips
To be intoxicated and smother
In this scent of love

He moves through me
Like lava
Destroying fear
Creating life as
He slowly loves me

Charlotte Wright

"Say My Name"

Say my name when
Your travels seem unnavigable
I'll help bring your soul home

Say my name when
The voices of this heavy
World become too loud
I'll help mute the drama
With my soul loving power

Say my name when
Your fears need to be sheltered
I'll dust off your crown
Shine it with the faith I have in you

Whispers

Say my name when
You need physical loving
I'll consume your mind, your masculinity
With luscious emotions

Say my name when
You roam into my eyes
I'll beam knowing you planted
Heaven into my life

Charlotte Wright

"By Candlelight"

By candlelight we become one
He slows his hands down
As he investigates all my curves
I can feel his heart pause
When I touch his pride
Thirsty for each other's love
We find our way by candlelight
I melt in his mouth and erupt in his hands
The beauty of this love is built on our mental
We balance and nurture the souls we are
Everything is put out there when we make love
Highlighted by candlelight

"I Find Myself Weak"

I sipped on your love for breakfast
I released a seductive blush
The world was at a hush as you delivered a mere hug
Sedated by the love felt deeply between us
I find myself weak yet ready to run back to back 5K's
Throughout my day I take breaks inside our love
I smile, cheesing, because you called to say hey
I'm all at the job dreaming, thinking.
This man has got me feening
My heart has been diluted by your raw emotions
I find myself weak yet ready to run back to back 5k's
Intoxicated by your mind
How you move me with silence
From the slight brushes to my rear end
You and I find us
A delicious love affair that has no end

Charlotte Wright

"Aftershocks"

I am aching to

Get you behind

Close doors

To walk across your spine

With sheer untamed desire

Every single inch of your flesh

Will be drenched in my rains

Of pleasure

My lips tremble as you conquer

My delectable fortress

Feeling your breath sauté

My flesh

I'm powerless, I'm paralyzed

By your controlled focus

Of me

Sending my body into deep

Out of control aftershocks

"I'll Keep It"

Right now
Right now I'll keep it
I'll water it and nourish
Your remarkable soul
I'll help fill it with peace
With warm mushy
Beautiful love
Right now I'll have my
Way with you
Entice you with the
Simplicity that flourishes in me
Right now I'll keep it
I'll keep you inside my heart
Close to the center
So I can feel you
Electrify my soul

Charlotte Wright

"Is It Just Me"

The loud silence between us

Says much more than the lips could

The mention of your name gives life to my skin

It rolls off my tongue

Sweeter than the act of making love

As I awaken from my sleep

You become the alarm clock I dare not ignore

Is it just me

or do you lust for me too

Is it just me

That doesn't have a clue

You and I collide in a place of just two

Waltzing in dreams from opposite sides of a room

Your rich voice is the therapy I seek

It mesmerizes my soul just to hear you speak

Whispers

Is it just me
That wants to explore the history in your eyes
Plant new stories to watch you smile
Is it just me
That is anxious to sleep
Knowing there's a possibility
Of seeing you in my dreams
Whispering, kissing and touching
Is it just me
That smiles among strangers
With visions of you just as you are
Or is it just me

Charlotte Wright

"A Beautiful Thing"

At the job I've thought on you
Visions of me devouring you
At break I heard your voice
Which lead to me daydreaming
Of when I see u in my bed
In the car I saw me and you
Smiled because that's where you gave me!!
On the drive I passed our park
Where we had relations in the dark
A beautiful collision of love and lust shared between just us
In the front room, on our couch
I reflect on how you arch your back
The shower holds its steam
Because of the way we do our thing
I crawl in bed to cuddle you and discover this right here
Is the most beautiful thing

"How Did You Greet Your Love?"

How did you greet her today?
Was it with beautiful intent?
How did you greet him back?
Did you speak to him and seal it with a kiss?
When you two are apart
Do you send naughty texts his way?
How did he react?
Did he say baby you got me craving your delectable parts?
As y'all ended the day
Did you as her King treat her as your worthy Queen?
Did you two invest even after you fell in love?
Do you echo their name when on bended knee?
How did you greet your heart's number one crush?

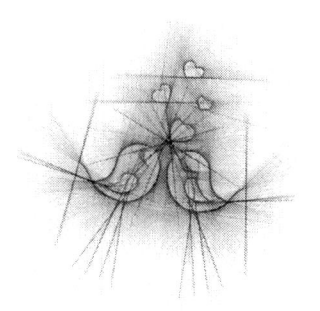

Charlotte Wright

"I Fantasize Of Autumn Nights"

The chill in the night's air
Evokes the romance within us
We belong to this season
Designed for stolen kisses and harmonious hugs
I fantasize of Autumn nights

You and I covered by crisp sheets
Underneath effervescent stars
Adorned by the same moonlight
That fills lover's hearts with sugary notions
I fantasize of Autumn nights

Taking in the Autumn air invigorates our souls
Golden leaves fall
Only to come alive beneath our physiques
Such beauty is captured, when
I fantasize of Autumn nights

"Bad Boy"

I only want him bad

At putting sweetness

On me

Like it was a crime

A crime to turn me out

A crime to turn me on

I only want that bad boy

The one that does me so

Right it feels

So

Incredibly bad

Charlotte Wright

"Grocery Store Bliss"

That moment at the grocery store
You bend over slightly to pick up a sack of potatoes
He slides his hand down your lower back
It feels so good
He is guiding you along the way
He knows he winning tonight
You turn to him, lick your lips and say

You must be peeling these muthas!!!:)

I'm invisible to you
A ghost with sensitive skin
Whom worships everything
That makes you ... you
A love that haunts only my mind
Ooh how I wish you were all mine

"Something"

Something something something
Is not complete within
Some voice inside is trying to reach me
It eludes me during my highest peak
But creeps back in during a sudden pause
It whispers things like girl something don't smell right
I think you're setting your heart up for the brink of death

Something something something
I suppose is warning me to walk away from tragedy
But the allure of glee truly excites me

Something something something
Wicked the voice says
But I pretend it's all in my head

Charlotte Wright

"I Crave"

To linger against your skin

To lose my thoughts inside your eyes

Feeling you in those depths that make my entire body quiver

I crave

To have your voice penetrate the simplicity of my being

I crave

To outline your masculinity with fingers and tongue

I crave

To be your hero, when you arrive home

Save you from the days that drain you mentally

I crave

Emancipate the anxieties and damage that lie just beneath

I crave

To take you in and hold you up on love forever

I crave

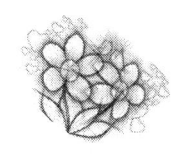

"With A Kiss"

When he kissed my lips
I felt my soul bloom
Alive and dancing this kiss of love
With just a kiss to the neck I swear
I flew through clouds and even laid with some angels too
The way he kissed my hand was charming
In that moment I was the star in a fairytale
Kissing my core made me break out in songs
Without words to express exactly
But he understood me perfectly
The kiss above my eyebrow infested me with security
I knew with that kiss, we'd kiss for eternity

Charlotte Wright

"Your Love"

Your love is like the moon across an Autumn night,
It fascinates upon the midnight hour
It pulls me in with every turn, giving my heart a race
Thoughts of you fill up my body
With warmth you've set ablaze
Your love is the dance of freedom
I've been chased by pain till now
I didn't know how blind I was
Until you enlightened me with sweet sights
Your love must be the heaven that awaits a dying soul
If so then take my breath away

"I Am"

I am the heart shape tattoo inside his chest
The oxygen that ripples through his veins
The voice that calms to embrace his secret scars
I am the peace that moves in his soul
And kisses dreams to have wings
The love surprised with patient moves
I am his exceptional novel
Read with joy and wonder
I am the meal he hungers and the drink he thirst
I am the soil to his seeds
Those roots survive with determined watering
These are the words he form and show me constantly
This I am

Charlotte Wright

"How Sweet Was The Kiss You Ask?"

When he kissed my lips
In fields of candy corn I napped
I danced with mermaids in seas of love
I chased lighting bugs to a crescent moon
How sweet a kiss this was
When he kissed my lips
I ventured to a land so enchanting
It housed rainbows and unicorns

"His Rose"

He planted seeds of love into her elusive ground
Placing her to shine in his vibrant sun
Watering her enough to show his love
He plucked the weeds from their roots
Fell to his knees to trim her hedges
Fertilizing her, watching her bloom into his rose

"How"

How did I exist without you before?
You seem to be water to me
The everything I need
To simply be
You're what my heart, my eyes, my mind and body desire
Every bit of you is my wants and needs
The smile that I don when I prance around
How do I go back to living without you?
I know for a fact, I never want to

"When Lovers Hands Meet"

Stabilizes my mind
Sends warmth down my spine
Encourages the beauty inside
When our hands meet in and out of sheets

Charlotte Wright

"Love's Wish"

Love's wish

Is to delight in every moment

To talk with vulnerability even when it's hard

Peel away fear as love trickles inside the mind

Love's wish

Is to walk into your life

Dance with you every morning

Skip with you through your day and

Cuddle you every night

Love's wish

Is to find you when you're blind

To open your eyes

Touch you and give you heavenly sights

Whispers

Love's wish

Is to shower you every day

Bathing you in beauty as it exfoliates the pain away

To lotion your soul with security

Love's wish is to taste the sweetness on your skin

To feel you tremble inside my walls

To kiss your lips and lick your love

Love's wish

Is to respect you

To appreciate your past and present

To allow you to be the human you are

Love's wish is to live there inside your heart

And grow amongst your spirit

To meet you at the crossroads of love

Love's wish is to journey with you forever

Charlotte Wright

"Pleasure"

The steam off his breathe onto my neck
Awoke passion in my toes
His face brushing against mine
Was him calming me down
Taking his time to savor his meal
There was no need for music because him
And I created our own slow jam
He pleasured me in places unphysical
Taking me aboard an eternal flight
To lounge amongst the pleasures of love

He tastes like homemade hot water cornbread
Mmm, I bit into him and
Could taste his old-fashioned soul

"Have You Ever?"

Have you ever loved someone
With every bit of your heart?
The way they stand without needing legs
As if they were crafted from Jesus tears
Each and every day seems too short
Every minute they slowly cultivate your dreams
Hearing their voice puts your world in slow motion
Have you?
Have you ever just really loved that one person
That person that's perfectly imperfect
Have you ever loved another with every bit of your soul?
Giving them all of you without regret
Without thought, without pause
Just breathing, living in unconditional love

Charlotte Wright

"What If We Took This Chance?"

What if we took this chance?
If we tripped over this thing between us
What if we held on to this high
Distributed from vibes?
What would happen if we skinny dipped
In what feels like love?
What if we took this chance?
I promise, I swear even to hold your hand
I'd stand in it, wade through it
Because I know you're the one
What if we removed the fear?
Or better yet, just keep it here
Let it be the light that leads us to see
What if you and I became we, lived on us and
Danced on the edge of trust?
What if we just took this chance?

"Chocolate Land"

As he returned to my chocolate land
Every minute, every second
I found myself captured by his treats
Lost for moments inside his mind
Wading through his delicious confections
Giving up my power willingly
Just to savor his completely
He brought waves of satisfaction
To my chocolate land
365 days he sweetly slaughtered my mind
365 days I sucked on his perspective slowly
Swallowing his convictions eagerly

"I want to crawl, crawl in and out your mind
Slowly, enthusiastically on the knees of love"

Charlotte Wright

"I Knew"

At first sight I knew
I felt you seep through my pores
Your eyes delivered fluency to my core
At that moment I craved for more,
More of your captivating soul
My spirit fell for yours within moments
Sedated by your genuine
I knew within that moment
I'd feed off you for the rest of my life

"Confessions From The Kitchen"

There I stood in all my insanity
Unplucked and spoiled
He stared at me with eyes that spoke of adoring me
Even with flour on my face

"I Need You"

I need you

Like stars need the charcoal

Of the night sky

To twinkle magically

Effortlessly

Like silent waters need

The rage of a tropical storm

To feel, to embrace the beauty in calm

I need you

I need you like the sea needs the moon

To shine, to dance, to marvel inside your

Magnificent waves

I need you

I need you

Charlotte Wright

"Beat Your Chest Baby"

Beat your chest baby

You got me

I'm on fire

The way you dance

In my mystical

Delicacy

Beat

Your chest baby

I'm high on you charisma

It's miles from average yet

Quietly humble

Whispers

Beat your chest baby
You're swimming in my mind
Biting my lip
Anticipating how you
Approach my diving board
Beat your chest baby
Or better yet
Allow me

Charlotte Wright

"There Are Times"

There are times

I think of you

That time

Is all mine

To rewind and catch

Visions of us

To inhale you in and keep you there

Exhaling sweetly

Knowing in a few

I'm inhaling again

There are times

I think of you

Whispers

Smiling because of what you do
There are places inside of me
Places that were tattered
Places only time, faith
And your unconditional
Love could heal

Charlotte Wright

"Touch"

His hand outlined my pride
A touch that pulled out my love
Melting inside my mind
After he touched me with sheer devotion
Touches that serenade my desires,
Yet cool my dramatic explosions
Wrapping his trust around my fears
Spoken words of how he feels

He touches me in places still cryptic to me
Waltzing in harmony together through the discovery
He held my heart inside his world
Writing our memoir for all to see

"The Rain, That's When I Want You The Most

Rain drops tap dance on the window pain
That's when I want you the most
Feeling the life in your simple touch
When it drips drops I long to snuggle
Entwined in soft sheets in the middle of the kitchen
Feeding each other off passionate love
That's when I want you the most

In the wee hours of the morning
The rain serenades the love that we make
The world paused when our bodies and mind
Become fully engaged in communication
Feeling all the desires you house for me
Lost under covers but our hearts give much light
You calling my love with every caress
Drowning in rain created by lust

Charlotte Wright

"This Man, This King"

Standing taller than an NBA center
Perched on courage, wisdom, faith, pride and
Inner peace
This man, This King
I bow to him not as his servant
But as the Queen he crowned me to be

This man has got me in a trance
Wanting to wrap more than legs around his head
He came from nowhere stealing
My heart devouring my entirety
Like a bowl of peaches and cream
I think the earth just moved up under me
by simply thinking on him
This man, This King

Whispers

His delicious lips got me drowning in heat
When he stares at me with those chestnut eyes
I give up on trying to push my emotions aside
Carried around on his shoulders and back
He looks at me to ask, is that all you got?
This man, This King

Charlotte Wright

"Snow Globe"

If I could capture that sparkle in your eye
When we held each other underneath the
Maple trees
How lovely words bounced back in forth
Penetrating each other's hearts
If I could capture the language that transformed into kisses
The quite seduction of your heart beating so close to mine
How you melt my soul with just your presence
If I could capture time and halt our precious memories
I'd capture it and place it in a snow globe

"One Day"

One day someone will understand
The courtesy in hello and good morning
One day someone will accept the purity of my tongue
They won't confuse my kindness with a flattering con
One day I will see my soul's reflection in another's face
Their sincerity will beautifully compliment my skin
One day someone won't use me to stroke their conceited ego
We'll stroke each other with actions from the heart
One day someone will unlock the password to my heart
He'll never need to reset it because he knows its true love
One day someone will see I'm as unique as my gap teeth
He'll love, treasure and keep me just as I am

Charlotte Wright

"No Thank You, I'm Full"

My baby has not let me starve

Breakfast, lunch and dinner

I'm filling up on his love

My mind has gained much weight

From all the consistency

He serves

Snacking and nibbling on

His honor and devotion

So no, no thank you

I'm full

I don't need any sides

My King's the main dish

And he's every bit my heart's wish

So no, no thank you, I'm full

"My Precious"

It is the jewel of my Nile

The ying to my yang

It circles my entirety

Beating and waiting for the one that's worthy

My precious

Go beyond her sleek curve

Touch my mind and ye shall find

A place to escape and live inside to dream

My precious you may get to meet

Only if I drown in your depth

I love you as the sun loves the breaking day

As the crane loves his freedom of water, earth and sky

Charlotte Wright

"Let's Sleep In Sorta"

Instead of cooking up breakfast

Let's just lay here, smooching

Under the scrumptiousness of

Egyptian cotton

As our liquid love simmer

Keeping the chill of Winter at bay

Let's sleep in, sorta

Stripping each other's arousals away

Slowly, emotionally mmm and

Perfectly physically too

Let's sleep in, sorta

Maybe wrestle a bit

I promise to resist just a little

Laying on your delectable chest

I rest

Afterwards I'm making you a

Sandwich

"Legs, Hips and Thighs"

I am the universe

The star that carries life

A planet made up of extensive oceans

A continent that cradles together many countries

I am more than my legs, hips and thighs

Touch my soil, watch how deep my roots flow

I am more than my legs, hips and thighs

My body is merely flesh warming a tantalizing soul

Walking, every step cracks like thunder

Talking, every word a world of meaning

Thinking of everyone as I am alright brushed aside

Singing, a chant

Only another true woman can distinctively hear

I am more than my legs, hips and thighs

Charlotte Wright

"Just As I Am"

From my nappy roots to my out of control curls
Even my extensions
My pecan flavored skin
And every inch of my voluptuous curves
He loves me, just as I am
The pride in my walk, how I bounce with such flair
He can't help but stare
From the pout in my lips to their full display
He seems to be amazed by the way it all lays
From the hope in my voice to the fear it sometimes utters
From the history in my eyes to the joy they never hide
He loves me, just as I am
All of my dreams and every vocal thought
He adores to see me simply as me
He loves me, just as I am

"Just Put It In"

To have you imprint
Your soul inside my odyssey
Was like giving birth to my divinity
I felt you come alive as you move precisely
Where you want to be
Traveling through my depths placing
Perfectly placed kisses
That made my skin beam with intensity
Taking in waves of my femininity
I hit high notes from your virility
Singing songs of love that live within me
My King, my heart I love it when you put it in me

Charlotte Wright

"I Want Some More"

You taste so scrumptious
I can't help but get the munchies
For your buttery soft skin
Beside, inside my chocolate factory
I want some more
I could say please
Biting my lips as I erotically tease
Whispers of seducing you escape from my eyes
I do declare, you've got me hungry for more
Longing to taste our future in your kisses
I want some more, tomorrow,
In an hour, for my lifetime

"Inside Our Love"

Inside our love we've captured inspiration
A mental and physical sedation of lust
Leaving confidence with every touch
With each kiss a chant of forever haunt the mind
Inside our love we stand tall
Able to push out all unspeakable fears
Inside our love we found a courage to heal
He feels safe inside her love
She feels safe inside his love

"I admitted to him I was numb,
Afraid and misplaced
He grabbed my hand firmly"

Charlotte Wright

"I Miss You"

When we've drifted off to sleep
Anxious to awake cause our love is on pause
Yearning for you in the depths of my dreams

I miss you
As we part to begin our separate day
Sickened by the hours that we have to be away

I miss you
Phone calls and texting just band aid my heart
Soon as they end my world falls apart
Face to face, heart to heart, my soul to yours
Is the only known cure

Whispers

I miss you
When your hands separate from my body
When your lips come up for air
When your skin pulls away from mine

And the only remedy is repeating,
Rewinding and trusting in our love

Charlotte Wright

"Emotionally Safe"

Suspended

Between

Hurt and hope

I walked onto

Your rope

Unshaken

Driven by your

Desire`

To make me feel

Emotionally safe

"His Home"

He planted his feet firmly on her foundation

Laying out his vulnerability

Living inside her heart

The place where debt held no value

Only love was collected, credited and spent

He discovered his destiny inside her many of rooms

Living and worshipping in her fortress

He used his mind to resuscitate her soul

His hands to hold her high with stability

Calling her love his home

"Confessions From The Couch"

I sat on the couch in boredom without the ruling hand

Entertained however by one seductive scene

The way he held my hand

Charlotte Wright

"His Chest"

As I lay my eyes upon
His stunning chest
I can hear him calling me home
To lay my worries on his masculinity
So he can make me feel safe
I can taste his honor and strength
As my tongue outline his pecs
My entire mind began to undress

"Sanctuary"

Your eyes are full of tranquility
I find solace in your laughter
I scroll your thoughts for serenity
Finding security in your tone
You my King, my dear heart
You are my sanctuary!!

"Ecstasy"

You release the seduction in me
Hard to maintain just holding your hand
It's something I'd settle for but you have to slay me
With your lips you sing songs to my sweet lips beneath
With your hand you caress my body
Like you were taught by Da Vinci
You breathe me in with every whisper,
Surprising my soul with pure ecstasy

"Devour"

I lust to devour your enchanting mind
Then put my lips around your succulent pride
You and me all alone
Pulling you into my wet odyssey
Taste the waves as you slide
Baby please devour me
Our mind and hearts connected as one

Charlotte Wright

"Delicious Kiss"

Your kiss has stained my mind

At Every Waking Hour

I find myself

Reminiscing on your evoking kiss

Inside I have melted

Five hundred different ways

Licking my lips just aching

For the hint of Nicotine

In your addictive

Delicious kiss

"Depth"

It's all about how far he lets me swim in his

And how far he wants to swim in mine

"We Don't Have To Take Our Clothes Off"

We don't have to take our clothes off
We can just lay here caressing
Undressed in our emotions
Tasting each other's thoughts
Stealing kisses as the moments come
We don't have to take our clothes off
We can just sip on the energy between us
As we walk around each other's hearts
Discovering the artifacts inside us

"This love taste so good,
That when we walk into a crowded room
Their first words are
mmmmmmmm"

Charlotte Wright

"Saving Her Hero"

She took the S from his chest
Laying his head upon her bosoms
She cradled him in love
Her lips bandaged his wounds
Each caress pulled tears from somewhere inside
Saving her hero in every corner of his mind

"Successful"

I find success in watching you smile
Bringing you peace
And catching your laughter
Aiming to always be successful

"Hope And Faith"

I am faith

You are Hope

Together we are

Seeds planted

In soil

Rich

With love

As we grow

Our roots shall

Thrive abundantly

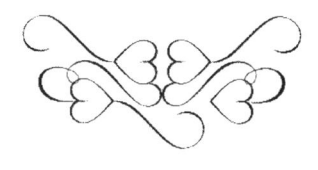

Charlotte Wright

"My King, My Love"

When you kiss my full lips

A lovely story starts to unfold

Laying across your chest is when I break free from your lady

To soar high being your girl

When you hold onto all my succulent curves

I feel the Queen in me passionately awake

My King, My Love you bring the heavens to me

"He made love to my mind

Every day

Waking it with encouragement

Penetrating it with his devotion"

"Nobody"

Nobody picked up her spirit quite like him
Embracing her fears with his
Nobody seemed to touch her fire
The intensity of her flames
Not just anyone could bare
Nobody touched her exactly
Where she needed to feel
Up to this point all others hands
Had only been numb
Nobody seemed to free her
From the desolate island where she laid bare
Till her hero showed up to blanket her with care
That is why her love is so fierce
Because nobody in this world had ever
Pierced her soul quite like him
Nobody…

Thank you

for taking this journey of love.

If you have enjoyed it,

please leave a review at

Amazon.com.

Charlotte Wright

Made in the USA
Lexington, KY
08 April 2016